T0162803

Dear Alison,
The Road Long Traveled

Pansy Ferrell Latta Dodson

WESTBOW°
PRESS
A DIVISION OF THOMAS NELSON
& ZONDERVAN

Copyright © 2014 Pansy Ferrell Latta Dodson.

Author Credits: Author of "Blessings and Hugs from the Sisters"

All rights reserved. No part of this book may be used or reproduced by any means, graphic, electronic, or mechanical, including photocopying, recording, taping or by any information storage retrieval system without the written permission of the publisher except in the case of brief quotations embodied in critical articles and reviews.

WestBow Press books may be ordered through booksellers or by contacting:

WestBow Press
A Division of Thomas Nelson & Zondervan
1663 Liberty Drive
Bloomington, IN 47403
www.westbowpress.com
1 (866) 928-1240

Because of the dynamic nature of the Internet, any web addresses or links contained in this book may have changed since publication and may no longer be valid. The views expressed in this work are solely those of the author and do not necessarily reflect the views of the publisher, and the publisher hereby disclaims any responsibility for them.

ISBN: 978-1-4908-2364-5 (sc)
ISBN: 978-1-4908-2366-9 (hc)
ISBN: 978-1-4908-2365-2 (e)

Library of Congress Control Number: 2014901164

Printed in the United States of America.

WestBow Press rev. date: 1/31/2014

The Slocums celebrate Christmas

This book is dedicated to Alison and her family. To Alison for giving me the reason for writing it and to Myrtle Frances, my daughter; her husband, Ken; and my grandchildren, Dan, Chris, and Alison. Each of them has brought purpose, love, and joy into my life as I have traveled this long road.

Special thanks and love!

Madeline F. Sparrow　　　**Violet F. Chappell**
Chapel Hill, NC　　　　**Wake Forest, NC**

A special thanks to my two sisters, who got me started and have traveled with me on this adventure. Violet died September 5, 2012. Madeline is still by my side, supporting and encouraging me.

~*~

Dear Alison,

You have always enjoyed hearing about the events in my life. So many times you have said, "Grandma, please write these things down so they will not be lost." Well, Alison, I have decided now, at the age of ninety, to start writing for you. I am thankful that so far my memory still seems to be intact.

~*~

In my first memory, I was about two and a half, and my grandfather was holding me. My father and mother both worked at the Golden Belt textile mill in Durham, North Carolina. My sister, older brother, and I stayed with my grandparents while our parents worked. Before I was three, my grandfather died of blood poisoning. He scratched his ankle on a crochet needle belonging to my grandmother, it got infected, and he died. I also had an uncle who died from smallpox. You do not hear about smallpox now.

There were two babies born after me, and both died very soon after birth. Seven years after me, Madeline was born. Since she was younger, she and I did not have much in common while we were growing up. Violet was a little more than two years older than me. Mother had five children who lived, and I was the middle one. The oldest was the only boy. The youngest child, Frances, was born thirteen years after me. Mother started to name the girls after flowers—the first Violet, the second Pansy, and the third Rose. Rose died as an infant, so she stopped naming us after flowers.

I remember going to Fuller Memorial Presbyterian Church with my mother. We sat in a small side pew. I laid my head in her lap, and my feet almost reached the end of the pew. I nursed milk from a round baby bottle with a large nipple on it. Most children nursed from the bottle until they were three or four years of age. There was no commercial baby food in 1922. I wonder what the mothers used for diapers in those days. A lot of clothes were made from feed sacks. These sacks came in colors and prints. They were sewn into teddies, slips, aprons, bloomers, and dresses. Feed for hogs, cows, and horses came in the bags. I think some of these bags could have been used for diapers.

I remember that at the age of five, I was in the nursery at church. Ms. Clara O'Neal was my teacher. In the spring, she gave each child a flower plant in a clay pot. She always gave me a pansy because my name was Pansy. I was a very active child. Now I would be termed hyperactive, but the word was not used then.

My sister and I walked two miles to church on Sunday mornings. One morning we arrived quite early, and there was no one there. We sat in our classroom for a while, and I became restless. I had always wondered where all the doors led to in the church. I got up and started to open the doors. I went up a winding staircase to the choir loft and stood looking out over the sanctuary. I saw a balcony up in the back. I went down from the choir loft through the sanctuary up into the balcony and looked down on the sanctuary. I went back to the basement to explore. I found the small kitchen and the furnace room and saw another small door. I opened the door and froze! There sat Mr. Bonnie Robinson, the custodian, on the commode with his pants down around his knees, reading the Sunday paper. I slammed the door and flew back to my seat and shrank up as small as I could.

Dear Alison,
As a child, I did not have toys such as you and
your brothers had. During spring, summer,
winter, and fall we played out of doors.
Without TV, children were more active.

We played hopscotch, had running and jumping contests, or made mud pies in jar tops. Later we had roller skates, and a few children had bicycles. We also shot marbles. We had no TVs, no cell phones, no iPads—not even a telephone! We had no radio until much later. In the winter, I learned to embroider at Mother's knee. I always liked coloring or drawing. Every Christmas I remember as a child, I received a coloring book, a tea set, and a doll. Of course, each child had a brown paper bag filled with an apple, an orange, chocolate drops, candy orange slices, hard candy, and raisins. Even today I remember the raisins were gritty.

Many times I would go across the road to play with other children without first asking Mother. When she missed me, she would break a switch off the elm tree.

Dear Alison,
Then came my school years.

I started school when I was seven. My birthday was in July, and when I was barely six, I was still small and skinny. Mr. H. E. Nickam, the principal of East Durham School, told my mother to keep me out another year. I was also the baby at home, and I did not want to leave Mother alone. The next year I had a new sister, Madeline. At seven, I went into the first grade and enjoyed reading, writing, and drawing.

Pansy in third grade   **Pansy in sixth grade**

I attended the East Durham School through the ninth grade. I completed the seventh and eighth grades in one year. When I graduated from the ninth grade, Ms. Beulah Davis, a neighbor, sent me a corsage of yellow rosebuds. *That was something!*

My first goal in life was to graduate from Durham High School. It was the only high school in Durham and a twelve-year school. The county schools were only eleven years (because students were needed to help on the farms). I graduated from Durham High with the class of '41. There were no school buses for the city schools. We got to school any way we could. We also had to pay book rent of two dollars a year. It was a financial hardship during the Great Depression. Many students dropped out of school to help their families. I enjoyed school. The East Durham School was only three blocks from home. The high school was three miles away.

Durham High class of 1941

Thinking of my school years reminds me of the hard economic times. Mother was active in the PTA. I would go with her to homes to check on families to see if they needed food and other things. One home I remember well. The family had several children, including a set of twins, the first I had ever seen. They were sleeping on the floor on pallets, using apple crates for chairs and tables. They needed fuel, food, and clothes. Somehow the PTA could get these for them. Many people came by our home to tell Mother what they needed.

Dear Alison,
This was written in later years and describes life
for many families during the Great Depression.

My First Funeral

It was a long, hot, sultry day in the late summer of 1929. I was sitting on the porch step making mud pies in old jar tops. I noticed Mrs. Perry calling my mother from her yard across the road. I sensed a note of urgency in her voice. As Mother started toward Mrs. Perry, I left the step and followed her. Quietly, I moved close behind them as Mrs. Perry said, "Lelia, did you know that Mrs. Burgess died this morning?"

Then, seeing me, they talked in low voices about her death. Mrs. Burgess was a tall, thin woman who had given birth to nine children. Seven were still living, ranging in ages from eighteen months to nineteen years. She had known only simple pleasures and few luxuries in her life. Her lot was hard and dreary. At forty, she was old before her time. During the Depression, Mr. Burgess seldom worked but was said to hang around with "loose women."

This was whispered among the neighbors. In fact, Dr. Ross himself implied that Mrs. Burgess's death was the result of a "bad disease" her husband had brought home.[1]

I was nearly seven, but I remember quite clearly the day of the funeral. My mother canvassed the neighborhood, gathering clothes for the Burgess children to wear. Our contributions were a blue shirt and striped tie from my older brother John, a green flowered voile dress from my sister Violet, and a red dotted-swiss dress and black patent-leather slippers from me. Having taken the borrowed items to the Burgess house, Mother came back to bathe and dress us.

I was wearing an outgrown pongee dress with a smocked yoke and tennis shoes that I had painted bright red (having sacrificed my best to Nellie Burgess on this

---

[1] In 1983, as I recalled the events of this funeral, I did not know the cause of Mrs. Burgess's death. After having a stroke, my mother came to live with me. She and I were in the kitchen having coffee one morning. No one else was in the house at the time.

I said, "Mother, what caused Mrs. Burgess's death?"

Mother looked around very quietly and whispered, "A bad disease."

I said, "Cancer?"

Mother, still whispering, said, "No, a bad disease. Her husband brought it home to her from loose women."

Times have changed since I was a child of seven. People did not openly discuss such subjects as sex, cancer, or "bad" diseases in 1929.

sad day).[2] We started walking up the dusty road to the top of the hill. Other neighbors came out of their homes to join us. Mother held my hand as we went into the old two-story house with a hall down the middle. We were engulfed in the heavy, sweet smell of carnations and an etherlike odor. The long gray casket was in front of a window with the green shade half-drawn. There were two designs, one of pink carnations and another of gladiolas, which had both wilted because of the extreme heat. Mother and I walked over to look at Mrs. Burgess. Her face looked gray, and her hands were folded on her waist. She was robed in a fluffy, light pink chiffon gown with lace ruffles around the neck and sleeves.

Mrs. Perry leaned close to Mother, whispering, "She looks better than I have ever seen her."

Mother smiled and said, "How nice it would have been if Mrs. Burgess could have felt the soft, pink gown."

"She probably never owned anything this soft and pretty in her life," said Mrs. Perry.

---

[2] My tennis shoes were painted red. I was always a very active child. One day when I was six, I found some red paint in my father's shed. I painted my shoes while they were on my feet. I wore tennis shoes in the summer. After lending my Sunday slippers to Nellie Burgess, I only had only the red tennis shoes to wear to the funeral.

Neighbors filled the room. Two younger children were running back and forth through the neighbors playing. Jessie Lee, the eldest daughter, barely sixteen, walked around with the eighteen-month-old baby on her left hip. To the two active children, she said, "Children, go out in the yard to play. There is no room in here."

Her mother's untimely death had shifted the burden of providing for the family's needs of cooking, washing, loving, caring, and sacrifice to the shoulders of Jessie Lee. Her fate was sealed. She would probably never have time to search for love, relationships, or personal happiness. Her only fulfillment could be in service to her sisters and brothers.

The Burgess boys were standing in the front yard while their father stood on the back porch talking to the men. A hearse and two family cars arrived from the funeral home. The boys carried the casket out of the front room, through the hall, and down the four porch steps. Mrs. Perry and Mother carried the two flower arrangements out to be placed on the casket. The members of the family were herded into the two shiny black family cars. The neighbors and their children were packed like sardines into three other cars. Few neighbors owned cars in those days. We rode for many miles up hills, down hills, and on paved roads and dirt roads through two counties.

Finally we drove into the washed-out driveway of a small white wooden church. Beside the church, gray tombstones of all shapes were protruding from the rough ground. Getting out of the cars, the men and boys walked to the front of the procession and lifted the casket and carried it to the grave. The funeral director opened the door of the family car. Mr. Burgess, wearing his only suit, the seat of his trousers shiny from much use, was wiping the sweat from his brow. He could not feel much comfort or solace on this humid, torrid day. He must have been overwhelmed with regrets and sorrow, realizing somehow that all of this was his own doing. Herbert, the oldest son, emerged from the car next, wearing my brother's blue shirt and tie. Then Jessie Lee crawled out, looking nice in my sister's voile dress, with the baby still straddling her left hip. Nellie followed the others, quite pretty in my red dotted-swiss dress and my patent-leather slippers. (I looked down at my tennis shoes, painted bright red.) Each garment worn by the Burgess children was easily recognized by the neighbors. I guess most of them were like me, sorting out clothes from each child in the neighborhood. Finally the family was seated around the grave, with the neighbors standing behind them. Reverend Harness stood and in a loud voice expounded on Scripture from the Old Testament and the New Testament. I thought his prayer would never end. The funeral director broke seven wilted carnations, giving one to each child to drop in the grave as a last token of love to their mother. Mr. Burgess, the men, and the boys picked up shovels and started filling the grave. Jessie Lee was crying softly, cuddling the baby's head into the curve of her neck, receiving comfort from the youngest child's affection. The grave was filled, the wilted flowers placed on top. The neighbors piled back into the three cars, stacked like sardines, to make the long journey home. We rode through two counties, on dirt roads and paved roads, up hills and down hills. Mrs. Burgess was free at last.

Dear Alison,
This is about a widow whom I have long admired. I
am happy that the choices for women are much better
for you than they were for women of the late twenties.

A Tribute to Lizza

I glanced over the morning paper as I finished my second cup of coffee. While reading the headlines and the current events, I turned to the obituary column. Scanning down the deaths, I read the name Lizza Garrard. I remembered back to eighty years ago when I was young.

On a cold January morning in 1938, Lizza turned her patchwork quilt back and got out of bed. She slipped on a cotton dress. She leaned over to pull a quilt over her two daughters who shared her bed. She slipped her feet into worn shoes, silently crossed the room, and closed the door. Lizza shuffled down the hall to the kitchen. She found an old newspaper, which she crumpled and stuffed into the woodstove. She added some kindling and slab wood, upon which she sprinkled kerosene to start the fire. After she rinsed her hands, she reached up to the shelf above the sink and took down a wooden bread tray in which she made dough. She spooned a generous amount of flour and pure lard, to which she added buttermilk. She mixed the dough with her hands, squeezing it until it was smooth. She shaped large biscuits, the size of saucers, and placed them on a pan and placed it in the oven. She poured Eight O'Clock coffee into an enamel pot, filled it with water, and placed it on the stove.

Lizza sat in her straight-backed chair, colored by many coats of chipped paint, and turned on the electric switch of her looper machine. She picked up the first bundle of unfinished socks, her shoulders slumped in toward the machine as she placed her right arm on the guard. She placed the open-toe socks on the small teeth of the wheel. They were sewn as it turned. As they moved around the looper machine, the tops were cut off. These tops, called loopers, were later braided into rugs. Once a week, Mr. Brown came from the Durham Hosiery Mill to bring more bags and pick up the finished socks. Lizza received a dollar a bag for her work.

Her gray eyes, squinted from years of strain, focused in on the small teeth of the looper. Black hair, cut straight at her shoulders, framed her face. She once was considered pretty with her black hair and gray eyes that danced with fun and intelligence. Her husband had died when the children were still small. Now Lizza had to feed and clothe five children. She rose early every morning to prepare breakfast and to work on the looper machine before the family came into the kitchen.

With the smell of coffee perking on the woodstove, the looper clicking in a steady hum, and, a generous dip of snuff in her lower lip, Lizza settled into her day.

When each child came into the kitchen, Lizza would leave the looper and give them a biscuit, saying, "The molasses and margarine are on the table. Clean up your dish when you are through."

Bob, the eldest son, entered and said, "Ma, did you iron my shirt?"

Lizza said, "Bob, it's hanging on your bedroom door."

A few minutes later, the daughters, Beth and Fran, entered the kitchen, shivering as they pulled on their dresses near the warm stove. "You'd better hurry or you'll be late for school," Lizza said. They hurried to eat, filling their biscuits with molasses and margarine.

Beth said, "Ma, your biscuits sure do smell good this morning."

Fran said, "Beth, is it Pansy who always talks about Ma's biscuits being so good?"

"Pansy and all of the children like Ma's biscuits and molasses," Beth replied.

"I even like molasses on my sweet potatoes," Fran said.

"Children, stop that chatter and eat, or you will be late for school. I need to get back to my looper machine. Mr. Brown will be here to pick up the bags of socks around five o'clock this evening," Lizza said anxiously.

Joey and Dan appeared sleepy as they stuffed their shirts into their pants. "Boys, you'd better hurry," Lizza said. "Here—take this biscuit and get a move on. I will never get my work finished with all of you poking around. Bob, help Joey with his shoes and get the others out to school. I'll never be able to finish these socks." The children each picked up another biscuit and ran from the house.

When the children came home from school, they would eat a bowl of pinto beans seasoned with fatback, and a baked sweet potato. This was their dinner. They seldom sat down together for a meal.

In front of the kitchen window, Lizza remained working at her looper machine. One afternoon, Fran ran into the kitchen shouting, "Ma, Joey is in another fight. He is rolling over the ground with Charles."

Lizza got up, pushed her chair back, and said, "That boy is going to get in real trouble." She ran to the door and called, "Joey, come home this minute!"

"Charles has Joey's ball and will not give it back," Beth said.

"Fran, get Bob and tell him to separate the boys and get Joey's ball," Lizza ordered. Fran found Bob, who went out and separated the boys and recovered the ball.

Bob said to Joey, "Ma is going to lay in on you if you don't stop fighting."

Joey answered, "Charles had my ball and wouldn't give it back."

"Why do you play with him?" Bob asked. "Charles is a bully."

The boys entered the kitchen. Lizza was back at the looper machine, trying to make up the time she'd lost dealing with Joey's fight. "Joey, stay away from that child," Lizza said. "You know he's trouble. I will never get this work done on time." She looked at the clock.

Lizza had few choices. She became trapped in circumstances beyond her control. There was no welfare or social services to help.

Days stretched into months and months into years. Lizza remained at her looper machine. The children were growing up. Bob was now married, and Joey was the youngest at sixteen.

One day, Joey came into the kitchen and said, "Ma, I don't feel good. I don't think I'll go to school today."

"What's wrong with you?" Lizza asked.

"My head hurts, and I hurt all over," Joey said.

Lizza said, "Take an aspirin and go back to bed. Maybe you'll feel better tomorrow."

Joey went back to bed and slept most of the day. He got up in the late afternoon, went to the kitchen, and ate a bowl of pinto beans and a baked sweet potato.

"You must feel better," Lizza said.

"I feel better, but I'm tired of that bedroom," Joey answered.

Later that evening, a friend, Walter, came by to see Joey. They laughed and talked for a few minutes. Walter said, "If you feel up to it, why don't we go out to the Starlight Lounge?"

"I feel better," Joey said. "That might be fun."

Lizza, hearing the conversation, said, "Where do you think you're going?"

Joey said, "I won't stay out late, Ma," and he left with his friend.

Lizza continued working at the looper machine, often looking at the clock. She was thinking that Joey should be home by now. The clock kept ticking. It was now after midnight. She was anxious, because Joey had never stayed out this late before. She got up from her work and called Bob. "Bob, I am worried about Joey. He went out with Walter and has not come in yet. Will you go and see if you can find him?"

Bob answered, "Ma, he will probably be home anytime now, but if it will make you feel better, I'll go out and look for him."

Bob got into his old Ford pickup and rode off. He drove down the road to the Starlight Lounge, where most of the teens hung out. The lounge was closed. Bob saw a few boys hanging around the building and asked them if they had seen Joey. One said, "Yes, he was here with Walter for a while, but they left earlier." Bob got back in his truck and drove slowly down the road. He saw something move on the right. He stopped the truck, got out and walked over, and heard a voice calling, "Help, help!" He saw Walter. Walter cried, "Help me. Don't leave me."

Bob asked, "Where is Joey?"

Walter, crying, said, "I think Joey is across the road in the ditch. A car hit us."

Bob walked across the road and saw Joey. He was unresponsive when Bob tried to rouse him. Bob had a terrible sense that Joey was already dead. He got back in his truck and went to the telephone booth outside the lounge and called an ambulance. The ambulance crew and police arrived. Joey was confirmed dead. Walter was transported to the local hospital. Bob dreaded going and telling Ma what had happened.

Back in his truck, he drove to Ma's house. As he entered the kitchen without Joey, Ma's expression froze. She suspected the worst. She could read the bad news on Bob's face. Bob whispered, "Ma, I have bad news. Joey is dead."

Lizza went into shock. Bob leaned over and flipped the switch off on the looper machine. Lizza screamed, "My baby! Why did he go out tonight? Why did he go out tonight? I blame Walter. Joey would still be alive if Walter had not come by."

Bob said, "Ma, Joey went because he wanted to. Don't put all the blame on Walter."

The following morning the whole neighborhood was shocked to hear that Joey had been killed on a highway near his home. Lizza's heart was broken. The neighbors tried in vain to console her. In deep despair, she continued her life of burden and toil. She had no time for self-pity. Even anger consumed too much of her energy. She still had children to support.

A few years later, Bob's wife died in childbirth. Bob brought the child back for Lizza to raise. As the granddaughter grew, she called Lizza "Ma" like the other children. Dan left home and joined the army. Fran and Beth went to work in a local factory. They both married young men from the neighborhood and started their own families. The daughters added a few luxuries to Lizza's life.

It was now 1955. Lizza still lived in the same four-room house with a hall down the center. A washing machine had replaced the looper machine. An electric stove had replaced the woodstove. On cool mornings the room was warmed by an oil heater. There was no need to bake biscuits the size of saucers anymore; the grandchildren preferred loaf bread. On the end of the kitchen table sat a TV—black and white, but a luxury for Lizza. Now she watched TV and tended her small garden in peace. She still missed the sound of children's voices and the hum of the looper machine.

By 1965, Lizza's family was no longer her burden. It was the dreaded disease of breast cancer. She went about her daily routine without grumbling or complaining.

It's unjust that one life should have such pain and so many burdens. When did she have time to pursue happiness or obtain peace? She could never find her identity with such constant pressure. Perhaps now she would receive her reward and peace.

I placed the morning paper on the table and set my cup in the sink. Too much time reminiscing. I marked my calendar: "Funeral, Wednesday, March 6 @ 2:00 p.m."

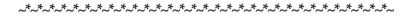

Dear Alison,
My life from seven to twelve years of age was routine.

Our neighborhood was filled with children. We lived on a corner. We played softball, football, badminton, and racing games. I also liked to climb a sycamore tree in our front yard. I would lock my legs around the limb and hang down and swing the smaller children, especially my younger sister Madeline. This was the age that I was first introduced to tobacco. On a hot summer day, I was sitting on top of a five-foot-high wooden fence. A neighborhood boy was chewing tobacco. I asked him if it was good, because he always had a chew in his mouth. He said yes. "Do you want a chew?"

"Sure," I said. He broke off a piece and gave it to me. I put it into my mouth. Suddenly the ground flew up and hit me in the face. I lay on the ground, stunned. When I got up, I went home sick as a dog.

Sarah, a friend, came and asked my mother if I could go with her to the park. The park was across the railroad tracks and belonged to the cotton mill. Mother told me not to go into the water. There was a pool for the employees and their families. Sarah's father worked there. I had never seen a body of water larger than a galvanized washtub. Sarah brought her sister's swimsuit for me. After we had changed into our suits, I saw all of the children in the pool. I ran ahead of Sarah and jumped right in. I went down, down, down, down. Then I went up, up, up, up. When my head popped out of the water, Sarah was reaching down. She took my hands and pulled me out of the pool. Then we went down to the shallow end. I had jumped into the deep end.

During the summer months, I would walk to town twice a week to the library to get books. Reading books was my vacation. My family never took a vacation. Daddy farmed. Summer was his busiest time. He never owned a car. He only had a mule and plow. During the summer, my sister Violet and I would go to the garden, pick peas or butterbeans, shell them, and sell them to the neighbors for fifteen or twenty cents a quart. I used my money to buy pencils, tablets, and notebooks for school. I was always eager to start school in the fall.

Mother had a piano. She could play and had a good voice. When I was the baby for seven years, she sang hymns as she rocked me. That is where I learned to love singing, music, and hymns. During hard times, Daddy swapped the piano for a crippled cow. I guess we needed milk and butter more than music. The cow became my and Violet's responsibility to take out in the countryside to graze. The cow walked slowly as we tried to lead her, but often she would get loose, and then she could run like a turkey. Violet and I would chase her all over the country. It must have been a funny sight, two young girls, twelve and fourteen, chasing a crippled cow. Thank goodness Mother did the milking.

We raised our own chickens. We had a mean rooster. One day before Easter, I asked my cousin Clyde, a year younger than me, to go in the pen and get us some eggs to hide. You know what happened. He came out screaming but was able to hold on to a few eggs. We hid them under the front doorsteps. When they were found, we both received a switching.

Since Daddy worked as a night watchman, Violet and I had to feed the hogs. The pens were almost a mile away from our home. She and I would carry two buckets each filled with ship stuff or slops to feed them. Often we would stop by the garden and fill the buckets with tomatoes or other vegetables.

Violet and I were close. We slept in the same bed together until I got married. No member of the family had their own bedroom, except my brother. Often there were three in the bed. There was very little privacy in most homes. I had a small trunk, given to me by a neighbor, Mrs. Letta Williams. I brought in her coal and wood after school each day. I kept all of my treasures in the trunk, the only personal item I had while growing up. I still have what is left of a scrapbook, made in the 1930s. It has valentines, cards, drink straws, and a few pictures still in it. I don't know what happened to the trunk.

When we got a radio, we would listen to *Amos 'n' Andy* and the *Inner Sanctum*, a scary program. Soon I began listening to songs. During this time I started watching Mother sew. I would sit in the bedroom window and help her pedal the old Singer machine. When I started before she was ready to sew, the machine would go backward. She would give me a hard look. I would take my feet off the pedal in a hurry. I loved to pedal the machine. Soon I learned to sew.

Mother had one pattern. It fit my sister, who was larger than me. Mother made both of our dresses from the same pattern. I started sewing to make my dress fit. I cut patterns from newspapers. The style was long-waisted, with gathered skirts and puffed sleeves, and trimmed with small lace. Soon I was making dresses like mine for other girls in the community. Their mothers would give me thirty cents, and I would go to S. H. Kress and buy three yards for another dress. Aunt Rosa came home from Tennessee, bringing me some red taffeta material. Mother made me a dress with a flared skirt. One cold morning I was warming my dress before the open fire; a draft from the chimney drew my skirt up the chimney and it caught on fire. It broke my heart. I loved that red dress.

I also liked to smell new shoes. We did not have many new shoes. I would carry new ones around in the box for days, smelling the new leather. Thinking about it now, it could have been the glue giving me a high. Today most shoes are made from man-made material.

On Monday mornings, we would wash clothes outside in tin tubs. Clothes were boiled with lye soap in a black cast-iron pot in the backyard. In the first tub, we had soap and a washing board on which to scrub them. The next tub was a rinse tub. The third tub had blue water to whiten the clothes. The last was a large dishpan filled with starch. Elmo, a neighbor who lived across the road, often came over to help us wash. I was eleven, and he was twelve. My older sister, Violet, washed in the first tub, I rinsed in the second tub, and Elmo rinsed in the third tub. He starched everything that came down the line. I did not want to drop our bloomers into his tub. If I did, he would starch them also. To tease me, Violet would reach around me and drop our bloomers into his tub, just to embarrass me. Then all the next week we were wearing starched bloomers. In our early years, Mother made our bloomers out of cotton material. They had elastic around the waist and the legs.

Elmo also had a pet goat that ate cans and plastic. When the goat died, all of the neighborhood children cried at the funeral.

My father raised hogs. Every late November or early December, after the first frost, he would kill hogs. I always hated to come home from school on those days, smelling the freshly cut meat and the skins boiling in the black pot to make lard. Mother boiled the liver in the house to make liver pudding. The hogs were killed, scalded, and scraped. They were cut into hams, shoulders, tenderloin, jowls, fatback, and so on. They were placed in salt and stored for the winter. We lived mostly on pork meat. We also had chickens and a cow. We canned vegetables from the garden for winter. My family had plenty to eat. The only beef that we ate was called bucket steak, similar to cube steak. I never had heard of broccoli in those days. We had turnip salad and cabbage. We ate dried beans in the winter a lot. At times, Daddy raised wheat for flour and corn for cornmeal.

In the summer, Violet and I would hand tobacco leaves to a person who would tie them on sticks to be hung in the barn for curing. Mother always insisted we work in the shade. She did not want us working in the sun. (She was a city girl; Daddy was a country boy.) We would receive fifty cents a day.

During the hot summers of my childhood, I would walk a mile to the garden to carry Daddy a half gallon of ice water. I would sit under a tree and wait for him to return down the long row. He would sit down for a few minutes and drink the water. Soon he would start plowing again, going out of sight down the long row. He loved the land. When I was younger, I would help him chop the weeds. Once in a while, I would chop a plant by mistake. I would stick it back in the ground. He knew this, but he never said anything to me about it. He loved his children.

Pansy and Violet, 1939

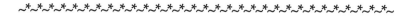

Dear Alison,

Memories of my teenage years were your favorites.

There were five teenage girls in our neighborhood. I was fourteen at this time. We were always laughing and talking together. One evening in summer, Freddie Pender came riding his bicycle down our road. He stopped when he saw us and started talking. He came down for several days, bringing us penny candy from his father's store. He soon became a friend. One day he asked if I would like to go to the movies. I said okay. He came early one afternoon. He wanted to take a picture of me. I wore a pleated blue linen skirt with a matching top. We walked two and a half miles to the Rialto Theatre, saw the movie, and walked home. It was still light. When we walked to my front door, Freddie asked me for a kiss. Well, I had never kissed a boy. I turned my head and offered him my cheek. This was my first date! A few days later I went to the store for Mother. The first thing I saw as I entered the store was my picture hanging up in front for everyone to see. That was the end of Freddie.

Later in the same summer, three teenage boys rode down our road. When they saw all the girls, they stopped in the middle of the road and started talking to us. Soon they were sitting on the porch with us, laughing and talking. Their names were James, Thomas, and Joe. All of us became friends. Thomas and Joe were brothers, both with dark brown eyes and black hair, quite handsome. James had wavy auburn hair and eyes the same color. He was a tall and lanky teen, always laughing and smiling. One day we were discussing birthdays. James asked me my birth date. I said July 18. He said his was the same day. I doubted it. He took out his driver's license. He was right. We both had the same birthday. We agreed to get in touch with each other on every birthday as long as we lived. He was fifteen, and I was fourteen. It was 1936. Our lives would touch for many years.

James started dropping by my home a lot of evenings, sitting around listening to the radio or talking to Mother or Daddy. He and I began dating. In those days, boys did not have cars, so couples sat in their living rooms listening to the radio. At nine o'clock, Mother or Daddy would come to the door and say, "It's bedtime." James would bring me a magazine or nail polish each time he came. He treated me like a queen. He worked at a sawmill. One night he brought Joe with him. Joe was leaving to join the CCC camp (Civilian Conservation Corps, 1933–1941). This program was started by Franklin D. Roosevelt to put young men to work. I told Joe how sad I was to see him go. James stood up and said, "If you hate to see him go so bad, why don't you kiss him good-bye?" Well, I still had not kissed a boy. I turned my cheek, Joe gave me a quick peck, and then he was gone with James. I did not see James for three years. He also joined the CCC. The camp paid a dollar a day, thirty dollars a month. The work was in forestry and building bridges.

Dear Alison,
Here is my childhood medical history.

Before I could go to school, I had to have a smallpox shot. Mother went with me to the health department downtown. When I saw Ms. O'Kelly, the nurse, take the long needle out of the drawer, I flew under the table in her office. She and Mother had to reach under and pull me out. I must have been screaming.

I had to have my tonsils removed. I had a lot of earaches, and my legs ached also. Everyone told me that after the operation, I could have all the ice cream I wanted. Mother went with me to McPherson Hospital on West Main Street. I was on a table when Dr. Facette laid a greasy cloth over my face and said, "Pansy, say, 'Heck, Mr. Doctor.'" I said it over and over until I was asleep. That was how he knew I was out of it. Several of my aunts sent me presents. I was the first child on either side of the family to have surgery, which was a big deal then. Two days later Dr. Facette came to my house to check on me. I was eating green pears that Violet and Virginia, a cousin, were handing me through a window. I was pretending I could eat only ice cream.

Our dental health was checked at school. Every two or three years, the county health department sent this old, bent-over dentist around to every school to check the children's teeth. His chair was placed in the back of the auditorium. Each child was sent up to see him. A teacher was always there to make sure that each child was seen. I did not have any problems.

In 1938, I was in the ninth grade. In February I started pinching my arm. I felt like I was on the outside of the schoolroom looking in. I felt like I was detached from the other children. Each morning I was so weak, I could hardly lift my arms to brush my hair. After several days, I started crying one morning. Mother asked what was wrong. I told her my arms were tired. She told me to lie back on the bed. She sent word to Dr. Ross, our family doctor. He came and checked me over and asked Mother a lot of questions. I still felt as if I was outside, looking in on the family. He brought Dr. Copperidge, a kidney specialist, down to my house the next day. They determined that I had a kidney infection. Dr. Ross told Mother that if she had not sent for him, I would have died in a few days. I was out of school for several weeks but passed with an A/B average. I have never had a kidney problem since.

Here I must say how loving and tender Mother was when one of us was sick. She knew how to make us feel loved and cared for. Even now when I am ill, I miss her hand on my brow and her tender touch.

James came one day and carried Mother, Violet, Virginia, Beth, Madeline, Frances, and me to Lake Mickey on a picnic. We wore shorts and halters to get a tan. We sat on the bank and enjoyed the food. Beth and I walked around the lake. We saw a lot of nice green switches. We thought about making grass skirts to tease Violet about her boyfriend being stationed in Hawaii. We broke a lot of the switches and stuck them up my halter and down in the halter until I was covered with the greenery. The next morning, I was itching around my waist and boobs. Beth came over, and her hands and face were broken out and itching. We had broken poison oak switches to make the grass skirts. Mother went with me to Dr. Shuler to get medication. I did not want to explain what we had done. I was glad that Mother was present at the time. She did not recognize the poison oak plant.

Dear Alison,
This seems like a good place to tell
you about my work career.

During the Christmas holidays, high school youth could work at the stores downtown. My first job was at Charles Department Store at the age of fifteen. I was placed at the front door, selling boxes of candy to customers. The candy, chocolate-covered cherries, was twenty cents a box. It was sleeting and raining, and I nearly froze to death each time the door opened. The next year I went to work at S. H. Kress, the newest five-and-ten store in town. I worked on weekends and during holidays. I worked full-time when I graduated from high school. I worked six days a week, eight hours a day for $11.88 a week. (Twelve cents was taken out for Social Security.)

I went to work at Liggett & Myers on February 4, 1942, as an hourly employee, making forty-five cents an hour. Men were being drafted into the army; women were hired to replace them. There was no air-conditioning in the building. The smell of tobacco was stifling. We were hired to destroy Piedmont cigarettes that were damaged in Pearl

Harbor during the Japanese invasion on December 7, 1941 to reclaim the government stamps on each pack that was destroyed. This saved the Company money. At the age of thirty-four, I was promoted to floor supervisor. In 1980, I retired in management as coordinator of seniority control. My responsibility was to work between a strong employee union, the Equal Employment Opportunity Commission, and a white macho management. Women were not paid as well as the men. The seniority system was complicated. The job came to me because my former boss retired and no one else knew the job. I was assigned an assistant. The young college graduate was making more than I was. This was in 1975. It was a good place to work, and the benefits were very good. I worked thirty-eight years, retiring at the age of fifty-eight.

Talking of work, I love yard and garden work. I love flowers, especially roses. I have always had a vegetable garden. I love the miracle of planting a seed and watching it sprout and grow. I have always been an outdoors person. Alison, you and your brothers, Chris and Dan, had a vegetable stand at the old well house to sell my excess food.

Alison and Chris at the old well,
selling my excess vegetables

Dear Alison,
Now I will go back to the time when James
returned from CCC camp, and my dating
years. In 1940, I was eighteen.

After James left for camp, I started dating boys from nearby communities. Mostly we double-dated in couples. I never dated a boy steadily. I would tell them to date whom they pleased—I was. I double-dated with my cousin Virginia. Her boyfriend brought a friend with him. Bob was four years older than me. He was quite like an old shoe. He started dropping around frequently. Meanwhile I went out with the girls. After three years, James came home from the camp. Now he had a car. He started riding by my home. Soon, he stopped and started talking to us. He and I started dating again. He and Bob both worked at night, having only one night off each week. When they had the same night off, it caused problems. Since we had no telephone, I would just go to the movies with the first one who came.

In 1941 at Christmas, James and his brother were going down our front steps after bringing me a cedar chest when they met Bob and his brother bringing me a large jukebox. Soon conflict arose between the two. One night James arrived first and we went out. Later Bob came and sat with my mother until James and I returned from the movie. Bob became very angry. Days later, Bob came to my house drunk. He threw down a picture of me, breaking the glass. He told me that I made him drink. Well, I went in the house and closed the door. A few days later he came and I would not speak to him. He came in and talked to my mother, telling her how much he loved me. Mother told him I was through with him. Later he tried to drive his car into James and me.

Meanwhile, I was dating other friends and going to meet their families. James was still in the picture. All the mothers and daughters in the neighborhood loved James. He was like a member of my family. He still treated me like a queen. However, I knew that James would drink. If I ever smelled whiskey on his breath, I would give him the cold shoulder. I knew that I could not tolerate it. My daddy would buy a bottle of whiskey each Friday. He could not bring it into our home; Mother would pour it out. When he came through the door after drinking, Mother would start arguing. She was all Scottish Presbyterian. She would not tolerate having whiskey in the house. Hearing this as a child tore my nerves up. Even though Daddy was over six feet, he never touched Mother. He would go in his room and go to sleep. He was Irish, humble, happy, teasing, and affectionate. (He loved his wife and children.) I never wanted to live this way. I knew James had marriage on his mind, but I tried to discourage him.

In June 1942, James was called to be examined for the army. He went to Watts Hospital for the examination. That same evening, a friend from work came by my home with a date. She introduced her date, Garland Latta, to me. He asked me if I had a date. I told him, "Yes, he has gone to be examined for the army." The next week, Garland called my grandmother's house and asked me for a date. Of course I said yes. He was handsome with wavy blond hair, blue eyes, and pretty teeth. He did not drink and was friendly and kind. He was from Granville County. The last thing that James said to me as he left for the army was "Pansy, when I get back, I am going to marry you, no matter what you say." I knew I could never marry him. Meanwhile, Garland and I became fond of each other. While we were dating, we went horseback riding and bowling, and we went to Crystal Lake to swim. Mostly we were with other couples. In fact, within four weeks he was talking of marriage. I told my sister Violet after our first date, "This is the man I will marry."

James came home on leave. He came to my home. He shook hands with Daddy, hugged Mother, and came to me, his chin quivering, and hugged me tight. I felt terrible. He asked me if I had a date. I said no. But I did have a date—with Garland. I had no way to get in touch with Garland to cancel the date. I asked James if he wanted to go to the movies. Again he asked me if I had a date, and I said no. I did not have the heart to tell him the truth.

We went to see Red Skelton, sitting in the balcony. I kept looking around. James said again, "Did you have a date?" Again I lied. I did not want to hurt him. Garland had come to my home, and when Mother came to the door, he said he knew something was wrong. He said he went to the same movie but was too upset to stay. James asked me to have dinner with his parents the next evening. I could not refuse him. We enjoyed the dinner with his parents. When we arrived at my home, we sat on the porch with other friends. Soon, Garland and his friends rode by. They stopped and came onto the porch. I was nervous. I didn't know what to expect. Garland laughed and talked to my sister Violet. Soon they left. When James asked me which one of the boys I had dated, I told him. James returned to the army.

H. Garland Latta, 1942
Age 22

Pansy Mae Ferrell, 1942
Age 20

Garland was scheduled to be examined for the army on September 12, 1942. We were married on September 5, 1942. We had known each other less than twelve weeks. He was exactly what I was looking for in a husband. He was eager to marry before he left. A friend drove us to Cheraw, South Carolina. We went into a Piggly Wiggly store; the manager took off his apron, went with us upstairs, and performed the ceremony. After Garland paid the justice of the peace, he had eight dollars left in his pocket and I had five dollars in mine.

Pansy and Garland, 1942

We did not have a honeymoon. We went back to my parents' home and lived there for two and a half years. During this time, James was serving time in Europe. On July 18 the following year, he sent me a corsage of yellow roses for my birthday. Of course this upset Garland. I could not send James a card or get in contact with him in any way. Garland was jealous of James. I never had a birthday that I didn't think about James and wonder how he was. For the next twenty-three years, I heard of him only through my family. James stayed in touch with them. I still felt guilty about not telling James the truth about marrying Garland.

Pansy and Garland in cousin Eunice's wedding, 1945

Garland and I saved money and moved into a rental house on Watts Street. We had enough money to buy furniture for five rooms. We were making less than a hundred dollars a week total and lived on a strict budget. I remember we had ten dollars a week for groceries. I was twenty-two, and Garland was twenty-four. He was not accepted into the army because of a heart problem. Garland sold his car. He needed tires; tires were rationed because of the war. The bootlegger who bought the car did get tires, probably on the black market.

Many food items were rationed because of the war. Fresh fruit was scarce, but one day I was lucky enough to find bananas. I made a banana pudding with meringue on top. I baked it in the woodstove and took it out with a wet potholder. It broke in half. I sat in the chair and cried.

We bought two bicycles and rode out on Saturdays with a lunch packed. Garland had never roller-skated, and he learned to roller-skate. We enjoyed the same things. Life was good. We were like two kids. We bought our groceries on Fridays, when we were paid. We would ride the bus loaded with large bags, exit the bus, and walk two blocks home. We lived there about three years, saving money for a home of our own.

Our first home and car

A house next to Mother's was for sale for seven thousand dollars. It was old, but the payments were low. We could afford twenty-seven dollars a month. We bought it and started fixing it up. I helped Garland replace half the roof. He made kitchen cabinets, and we made a small breakfast room out of a pantry. We laid down blocks of linoleum in the kitchen. For months, we were scrubbing up the black glue that oozed between the blocks. A bookcase was built beside the fireplace in the living room. We covered the wood walls with Sheetrock. We were cooking on a woodstove. You could not buy an electric one because of the war. The bathroom was on the back porch. There was only a commode; we added a bathtub. Garland made the porch into a sunroom. He also built a trellis over the driveway and planted yellow climbing roses on either side. The original house and garage had been built in the early 1920s. Garland took the garage down and built it back the same size it was. When we got a car, the garage was too short for the car. One day when I returned from town, there were five young men in our home, painting the new walls of Sheetrock.

We were in our midtwenties. These were the happiest days of our lives. Garland and I were now active in Fuller Memorial Presbyterian Church. Our friends were from church. It was after World War II, and we were in a young-adult class of fifty members, all young couples. They became our friends for life. Each weekend we got together at one of our homes. We did not have money to eat out. We played canasta for entertainment. Most of us were working toward a home and family.

Garland's father had a stroke and came to live with us. Two years later he had another stroke and died. Garland's brother Walton moved in with us. In 1948, I was having problems with my right side. I had never had a medical examination. I was in such pain, I went to see Dr. Lewis McKee. He left his office and led me down the hall to see

Dr. Edwin Robinson, a surgeon. The next day I was at Watts Hospital.

Garland was distraught. I tried to keep him cheered up. At this time in my life, I was reading the Bible through. I was not afraid. I was told that I had masses in my right side. It turned out to be endometriosis. During the operation, a large mass was also found on my left side. Part of each ovary was removed. Dr. Robinson told us that if we wanted children, we should not wait any longer.

Within two years I was pregnant. Garland and I were excited about a child. We started saving money for a baby bed and other items we would need. I was now twenty-seven. I never felt better than when I was pregnant. One day I felt a tiny movement, like a feather. We were ecstatic. One night when I was five months along, I woke up and knew something was wrong. We called Dr. Rodwell, and she met us at Watts Hospital. I had a miscarriage. Our hearts were broken. Garland told the doctors that he could not understand it. Other people had babies and did not even want them. Why could we not have a child? Of course I was depressed. The beautiful bassinette, given to me by friends at work, was donated to our church nursery. Maternity dresses that I had made were sent to a friend in New Jersey who was also expecting. I never became pregnant again. I did not have enough ovaries to carry me through the pregnancy.

One large door closed in my life. Life went on.

At this time, Garland and I did not have a car. After the miscarriage, we decided to buy a car with the money we had saved for the baby. Garland went off and came back in a 1940s light blue Studebaker. I could not tell the front from the back. The only items we ever bought on time were a house, a car, and a piano. If we did not have the cash, we did without. Garland's brother Walton moved out of our home and married his girlfriend, Frances. She became pregnant the first year. On September 6, 1951, they had a baby girl. Five and a half months later, Frances died quite suddenly. After the funeral, Walton brought the baby and placed her in my lap. He said to the baby, "Here is your new mother."

God opened a door in my life.

Myrtle Frances Latta came to live with us in February 1952. She was born September 6, 1951.

Garland and I took care of Myrtle Frances as if she was our own. Later Walton married again and had a son, but Myrtle Frances stayed with us. Garland and I were still saving money for a new home. I sewed all of my clothes and even made my hats. In those days we wore gloves and hats to church.

In 1956, we built a brick ranch-style home on Horseshoe Road east of Durham. We enjoyed landscaping the yard and had a vegetable and rose garden.

Home on Horseshoe Road

Myrtle Frances still lived with us. I always told her that I was her aunt. She knew the truth about her mother. Her father lived across the road from us. During this time, we bought a piano, since all of us loved music. Garland, Myrtle, and I took piano lessons. We kept the piano stool hot, sliding on and off to practice. Of course, Myrtle was the only one who stayed with it for twelve years.

Now we were able to take vacations and mostly went to the North Carolina beaches. Once we went to Florida. We covered most of the sights and had our first filet mignon for $2.50. We also went to Canada and to New York.

Life was good.

In 1957, Garland was thirty-seven and having problems breathing. Walking up our driveway with the paper each morning, he struggled for breath. After seeing a doctor, he was told he had emphysema. Over the next several years, Garland's health grew worse. We both still worked. Myrtle Frances was in school, and we were still active in church. We were blessed with many friends. The church was our life. We both taught Sunday school and sang in the choir. Garland was a Scoutmaster, and we became advisers to youth groups when I was twenty-six and he was twenty-eight. Some of my happiest memories of church are of the young people who are still my friends. This lasted for twenty years at Fuller Memorial Presbyterian Church.

Garland's breathing took a toll on his heart. Each winter he had pneumonia several times. He began to have heart failure because of the strain. He died at the age of forty-five. At his death I felt like a mule had kicked me in the stomach—such a hollow feeling. We had always been together. I was forty-three and Myrtle Frances was fourteen. I legally adopted Myrtle Frances at this time. A wonderful chapter in my life ended.

Another door closed.

1943

1947

Pansy and Garland at church, 1958

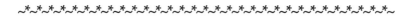

Dear Alison,
I need to insert the following story into my memories
at this place, since it is about Garland and faith.

Mother's Advice

As a child I attended Fuller Memorial Presbyterian Church and Sunday school with my mother, sister, and brother. Through the years, Mother was forced to remain home because of the illness of my younger sibling Frances. My older sister, Violet, and I would walk two miles each Sunday to church. We continued this until Violet became sixteen. She quit school and went to work at the local hospital. She worked on Sundays. As I had no one to walk with me, I stopped going to the Presbyterian church. I went with different friends to their youth groups at the Baptist and Episcopal churches. As a child, I prayed for members of my family. I always had an inner sense of God's presence. From my late teen years until I was married at twenty, I did not attend church.

In my early married years, my husband and I went to spend the weekends with his father in Granville County. My brother, younger sisters, and mother were still active in church. In 1945, on a Saturday evening, Mother called and said, "Pansy, why don't you and Garland meet me at church tomorrow?"

I asked Garland and he said, "I don't see why we can't." So the next day, Sunday, as we stepped down from the bus, Mother was standing on the corner in front of the church waiting for us. It was a little awkward, going into a group of strangers. They were mostly young men returning from service in World War II, bringing their wives. In a few weeks, we had made friends with several of the couples. We renewed our profession of faith and were accepted into the church. We became active in the choir, teaching juniors and advising youth. Garland was a Scoutmaster. The church became our lives. Our best friends at the church became our family.

Through the next twenty years, our lives were blessed through our church friends and family. We were young couples starting families and buying homes, finding our way into the world. We ate with each other or cooked out. Few of us had money to eat out. The fun and fellowship we shared could not be bought with money. All the while, we were growing in faith and fellowship.

Barely forty-five years of age, Garland died of heart failure. The night of his death, I returned home from the hospital at midnight. My yard was filled with men and cars. Every deacon and elder from our church was there. They did not want me to enter a dark, lonely house by myself. They were there to show me love and support.

This is 2013, and I am ninety-one and living in a different county. The few of our early friends who are living stay in touch.

Fate brought me to Orange County in 1968. Here I am active in New Hope Presbyterian Church. I also have made friends and become part of another wonderful church family.

How thankful I am that we took Mother's advice and went to meet her at church that Sunday morning. Our lives changed. We have enjoyed the blessings of fellowship with God, many wonderful friends, and church families that will last through eternity.

Sometimes I wonder if we would have gone back to church if Mother had not asked us.

Dear Alison,
After a death, there is always a time of
adjustment to changes in life.

The next few years were years of adjustments. Our home was paid for at Garland's death. I owned a rental house. I had a good job. Myrtle Frances was in high school. I was still active in church. I tended my garden. But life still seemed empty. Days and nights seemed long. There was no one to enjoy seeing the first rose or the first sprout of a seed in the garden with me.

Life went on …

Dear Alison,
A new chapter begins. Another door opens.

When I became a widow, I would not look at a man. I knew that I might be vulnerable. I did not want to mess my life up with the wrong person. Several men called me, but I was not interested in dating. Vincent Dodson, a friend, worked at L&M, where I worked. He and I graduated from Durham High in the same class. He would come by my office to tell funnies. I would ask him if the funnies were dirty; if so, I did not want to hear them. I did not tell or listen to dirty jokes.

One day he asked me if I would go out to dinner with him. I could trust him not to get fresh with me, since we were friends. I knew of too many widows who went out and men tried to get fresh with them. I went out with Vincent. He was a good-looking, neat person. He was always well dressed. He drove a sky-blue Ford convertible. We went to the Angus Barn for dinner. I was nervous. I felt guilty, thinking about Garland. While we were eating, some of the top officials from L&M came in. The next morning, three thousand people knew that I had had dinner with Vincent. So much for privacy!

Vincent and I dated for several months. He drove me and my daughter to meet his aunt and his two sisters. Vincent had a very nice family: Aunt Bessie and sisters Dolores and Genevieve. None of them had ever married. After several months, Vincent asked me if I thought I would like to live in Orange County. I knew that Vincent would take a social drink. This was something I did not know how to handle. The only reason I had even dated him was that he was a bachelor. I would not look at anyone who was supporting another family. Before I dated Vincent, I had talked with my minister about him. My minister said I was still young and had a lot of life left to share with the right person.

As Vincent talked more about marriage, I asked him to talk to his family and see how they felt about us getting married. His family was very close, and I did not want to disrupt them. It took him a week to get enough courage to approach them with the subject. On a Saturday evening when he arrived, he told me they were happy for us. The next day, they went across the road and picked out a place for us to build a house. I took this as their approval of me. Vincent brought house plans for us to make decisions.

I was concerned about his social drinking. Different people finally convinced me that at the age of forty-four, he had never had a drinking problem, and it wasn't likely to happen now. He also knew of my concern. I went out with Vincent only because I thought he was a confirmed bachelor. I thought I would not get involved. In fact, I suggested he ask a girl who worked for me out on a date. He did and said it did not work out. I asked him one day if he was ever going to get married. (At this time my husband was still living.) He said he would if he met the right person. It never crossed my mind that he and I would later marry. I always knew that if he did decide to marry, he would make a good husband. This I observed as a friend.

After eighteen months of courtship, we were married on April 27, 1968. This time I married in St. Thomas More Catholic Church.

**Pansy and Vincent's wedding at St.
Thomas More Catholic Church
April 27, 1968**

Vincent was from a Catholic family. He was raised in Catholic schools until the ninth grade. This was a disappointment to my minister, but I knew it would make Vincent's family happy. I was married in a Piggly Wiggly store the first time, and we were as happy as could be. It was not the place but the commitment each of us made. There were more men at this wedding than women. I think all of Vincent's friends wanted to be sure this bachelor was in fact getting married. My daughter was the maid of honor. After the wedding we went to Litchfield Beach for our honeymoon. I moved to Orange County into our home across the road from Vincent's family.

Vincent and I enjoyed our life. He worked on the farm, mending fences with Aunt Bessie. They were raising beef cattle. I was busy in the yard and garden. Myrtle Frances was attending Lees-McRae College. God opened another door.

Life went on … Life was good!

Vincent and Pansy, 1972

Pansy and Vincent

1973

Dear Alison,
This is the time that James showed up in my life again.

On a day in late spring, Vincent and I were on our way to Atlantic Beach for a vacation. Vincent stopped at a service station to get some gas near Havelock, North Carolina. I had heard that this was where James lived. I looked in the telephone book in the phone booth and found his number. When we arrived at the motel, Vincent said, "Why not call him?" Vincent knew the guilt that I carried.

After dinner, I called James. He answered the phone. I said, "James?"

He said, "Is this you, Pansy?" I told him that my husband and I were at the beach, and I asked if he and his wife could come see us. He knew that Garland had died and that I had remarried. He said, "We will come right over." I had not seen James in twenty-four years. He still looked the same. He asked for a hug when he came in. He and his wife stayed a good while, all of us talking about our lives. He and Vincent got along very well. He asked for another hug as he left. From that time until his death, we stayed in touch with each other.

The first Christmas card that I received each year was from James. One year I did not receive a card. After Christmas his wife, Inet, wrote me a letter to tell me he had had a stroke, a heart attack, and other health problems. From that time on, each Saturday morning at eight o'clock, I would call him or he would call me.

We were the best of friends. My sisters and I stopped by their home on the way to the beach and went out to lunch with them. Later James and Inet came to Chapel Hill and had dinner with Vincent and me. One Saturday morning during our phone talk, James said, "Pansy, maybe we made the right decision after all." Hearing him say this lifted a load from me. I felt he was forgiving me for hurting him years ago. A few years later, at his death, my sister, her husband, and I went to Havelock for his funeral. I still send notes of cheer each month to his wife, who is in failing health. James was one of the sweetest people I have ever known. I learned later that he had been an alcoholic during his life. I remember him at the age of fifteen. He treated me like a queen. He brought me nail polish, magazines, or candy each time he came to see this fourteen-year-old girl.

Dear Alison,
A new chapter on this road long traveled.

Vincent and I enjoyed our home in Orange County. He was still attending the Catholic church with his family. I was active in New Hope Presbyterian Church. We made friends with several couples our age. Myrtle Frances graduated from Lees-McRae College. She married Charles Kennedy Slocum. In 1976, my first grandchild, Daniel Gregory Slocum, was born. My life began all over again. Three years later, I had another grandson, Christopher Bradley Slocum. Eighteen months later a beautiful granddaughter arrived, Alison Lindsay Slocum. Our lives were complete. Vincent and I went to games, concerts, recitals, graduations, and so on. We were fortunate to be close to our grandchildren. They spent most of their summers with us.

Life was moving on.

Pansy and Alison, 1987

Alison, Dan, and Chris Slocum, 1986
Grandchildren as the Three Amigos
(costumes made by Pansy)

In 1980, I retired from L&M at the age of fifty-eight. Vincent worked on for five years. I had a greenhouse. I loved planting seeds and rooting azaleas in the greenhouse. I worked one day a week with H&R Block, doing taxes. I also took a real estate course and got my Realtor's license. I volunteered with Volunteer Income Tax Assistance, working as site coordinator in Hillsborough during tax season for fifteen years.

Life was good.

In 1981, my mother had a stroke and came to live with us on August 5, Vincent's birthday. She was with us eight and a half years. During this time, I learned a lot about her life. This is when she told me about Mrs. Burgess's death. She was busy making latch-hook rugs. She learned to use a walker and was able to get around, going up and down stairs. She was always easy to deal with (not like she was in my childhood). I was the middle of five children. I was the only one who was able to take her at the time. Vincent was always good to her. She loved Vincent. I enjoyed this special time with her. My sister Madeline took Mother to her home for the last two and a half years of her life. She died at the age of ninety-eight.

I was now seventy. Vincent was now retired. We still enjoyed being with friends, going out to eat, and entertaining on our large porch or at the pool. I was still busy in the garden. Vincent was still busy on the farm. We went on vacations from Canada to Key West, and many times to the North Carolina coast.

Life was good.

1983

Vincent and Pansy fishing at the Outer Banks

Vincent on his tractor, 1984

Dear Alison,

I am nearing the end of the road long traveled.

After working on fences and doing mechanic work for many years, Vincent was having problems with his knees. In October 1988, he went into UNC Hospital and had both knees replaced on the same day. He was in the hospital for thirty days. Mother was with us during these days also. The rehabilitation was difficult and slow. He stopped raising beef cattle. He was not able to keep up the fences.

A few years later, he had a heart valve implanted. His knees were still giving him problems. Meanwhile, he developed prostate cancer. This was kept under control with the help of Dr. Whitehurst, a urologist. Vincent and I still enjoyed our many friends, going out to dinner each month. Our friends and family enjoyed fellowship on our nice porch and pool. Life was good even at this age. Vincent's aunt Bessie died in 2000 at the age of ninety-five. She was a wonderful person and a very devout Catholic. In 2001, his youngest sister, Jenkie, died. His sister Dolores got a diagnosis of Parkinson's disease. Vincent was also having problems after second knee replacements. That left only me to take over the responsibility for Dolores's care. I tried to hire different people to take care of her in her home. That did not work out. She needed skilled care and was a patient at Brookshire Nursing Home in Hillsborough. Meanwhile, I had hired a certified nursing assistant to help take care of Vincent. He could not walk. He also had an operation on his spine.

Challenges kept coming with age. We were now in our eighties. I had a hip replacement in 2007. Vincent's condition was getting worse, and Dolores's condition was deteriorating too. Our CNA, Tanya Whitted, came to live with us so Vincent could remain at home. She or I would go to check on Dolores each day to be sure she was looked after.

Vincent was a sweet, thoughtful husband. He did not have a lot of patience, but he did have a lot of wit. Everyone liked him. When he became depressed, I would remind him of all the wonderful things we had going in our lives and how good God had been to us. He liked to watch cowboy movies. He could not turn over in bed by himself, and I slept on a cot in the room with him to be near him. One day, he told a friend that the best decision he had ever made was to marry me. That was the best compliment I had ever received. During these days, I understood what love really means. Each day I felt that Vincent and I loved each other more. I loved him not only as a wonderful husband but as a mother loves her helpless baby. I now look back at my life and see why God has brought me to this place in time to be here for Vincent and his family. Dolores died in April 2010. Vincent died on January 10, 2012, at the age of eighty-eight. Another door closed in my life.

During our last years ... Pansy and Vincent

Pansy and Vincent, 2002

Pansy and Vincent

Pansy and Vincent

2006

2007

The grandchildren are through college and into adulthood. Daniel is back from Germany and is now in Canada: Christopher graduated from Bowling Green and works in information technology in Durham. Alison is working for Memorial Sloan-Kettering Cancer Center in New York. Myrtle Frances and Ken live across the road in the Dodson home place. My sister Madeline Sparrow is my only family left. I still live in my and Vincent's home. Tanya is still with me. I am now ninety-one years of age and nearing the end of the long road traveled.

Tanya, Vincent, and Pansy, Christmas 2007

Dear Alison,
Now is the time to wind up my memories. I wrote
this piece after Vincent's death on January 10, 2012.

After four knee replacements, one knee repair, a heart valve implant, back surgery, and prostate cancer, Vincent was confined to bed. With the help of a certified nursing assistant, who lived in with us 24/7, I was able to keep my husband at home.

I had a cot in his bedroom and was near him night and day. If I had to run an errand, I rushed back to be with him. When I grocery shopped, I'd look around, trying to find the Pepperidge Farm shortbread cookies that he liked.

In the next four years, I could see small ways in which he was getting weaker. Tanya and I would have to pull the pad under him to turn him over in bed. He lost the use of his limbs. I remember Vincent as a tall man, six foot three inches, broad of shoulders, and strong, splitting logs for the fireplace and hauling wood in his pickup truck. He was happy working with his tractor and farm equipment. He could always find outdoor chores.

Now his body was sore and tender, and he could not stand to be touched. In the late spring of 2010, he stopped eating for six weeks, taking only sips of liquid. His body wasted away. This seemed to be the beginning of the end. I started planning his funeral. During this time, I pleaded with him to try to eat. He did start trying to please me by eating a little. I was asked if I wanted hospice to come in and help. I said no. I knew Vincent would give up if he heard the word *hospice*. He lived another eighteen months. Many mornings my pillow was damp from quiet tears that had slipped out during the long nights as I prayed for both of us.

Each evening after dinner my sister Madeline and I sat with him to watch *Wagon Train* or a Western movie. For five years this was our routine. Vincent, a polite person, thanked everyone for each favor or service. He was an outdoors person who loved to ride his John Deere tractor over the pastures, mend fences for his Angus cattle, and fish in the ponds. Vincent's friends were fed delicious steaks from his grill. His grandchildren loved him for his wit as he told about his time in Europe during World War II, recited the limericks he picked up while in the service, and talked about the different phrases used by his comrades.

Like a helpless infant he lay, needing me to care for him as if he were a baby. I saw to his every need. My heart cracked each time I looked at him. I always tried to put a happy face on and be cheerful when I was in his room. When he became depressed, I would recall all our blessings—that we were together in our eighties, still in our own home. A few times when he became confused and thought he was in Richmond, where he had cousins, I would say, "Let's take a nap; then we can start for home." When we woke up, he had forgotten about being lost in Richmond. I could calm him when he became agitated or refused to take his medication. Vincent tried to please me.

In early December 2011, he developed pneumonia. From 225 pounds, he now weighed 160. For several days, Tanya and I sponged him when his body was wracked with high temperatures. From then on, it was downhill. I prayed that he would live through Christmas, and he did. I prayed he would live through the New Year, and he did. As January 2012 began, I could not fight for him to stay with me any longer. My sister said, "He does not want to leave you."

I said, "I am not ready for him to leave me either." Yet I realized it was God's time for him. It was not easy for me.

During the weeks that followed, I entered my "zombie mode." I took care of the arrangements: services, burial, and reception. Taking care of business kept my mind busy. I did not have time to mourn.

Six weeks later, grief caught up with me. A heavy sadness settled inside. I felt like a leaf, fluttering around, detached from the branch but unable to reach the ground. I had no purpose for living, no direction in which to go. No one needed me. As I write this, my tears are flowing. I can hardly see the keyboard. This happens each time I sit to write. My world changed drastically. I still smile and laugh, but inside, my heart is crushed without Vincent. I know it is said that "Time heals all things." I am ninety-one, and I don't have that much time left to heal from this grief.

Spring is almost here. That should calm my spirit. I am a gardener. That is the only place that I feel peace. My connection with God and nature are the hope I hang on to. I am praying that soon this lost leaf will find something on which to anchor. Each morning I am in the garden planting flowers in the perennial bed or checking the seed bucket to be sure I have enough seed for the vegetable garden. Gradually the heaviness inside me lightens. My tears are beginning to slow down. God has heard my prayer and is lifting this weight from me. I will keep all of the wonderful memories that I shared with Vincent. He will always remain part of my life.

I watch each day to see the cucumber and squash seeds sprout in the garden. Vincent is near, enjoying the miracle of another spring with me. The roses are budding. Vincent would bring the first rose of the season and the first daffodil that bloomed into the house for me. He was a romantic at heart. I will miss the many ways he expressed his love for me. I am thankful for the life that we shared.

After five years of being confined to his bed, Vincent died on January 10, 2012. You have heard, "Death begins at birth." There is a lot of living between birth and eighty-eight years!

Our last picture

~*~

Dear Alison,
This is a message that I wrote in January about life.
It is titled "A Brief Summary of My Life." I thought
you might like it. It was printed in my former
book, Blessings and Hugs from the Sisters.

~*~

New Year's Reflections 2001

My, how the years have flown so fast.
The older I get, the shorter they last.
In the days of childhood, they seemed so long,
I thought I would never be big and strong.
In the days of youth, life was happy and bright,
Never a worry through a long, dreary night.
Then when romance and love came my way,
There was not a care in the world to me that day.
Then came the serious responsibilities of life.
I became a homemaker, a mother, and a working wife.
My, how the time flew quickly by.
Now I am past the age to retire.
How thankful I am through all of this time
To have a Savior who is always mine.
Through struggles, strife, joys, and love,
Sickness or death, I had strength from above.
No matter what the New Year brings,
God will be with me through everything.

~*~

Dear Alison,
Now is the time to seek God's purpose
for the remaining years.

~*~

I am still writing messages of cheer for shut-ins each month. Since spring is here, the garden is calling me. I would like to plan a trip to the beach with Madeline to watch the waves roll in and out. I try to stay in touch with the grandchildren. I still enjoy reading and watching the many birds in my yard. I sit and meditate on the long journey that God has allowed me to enjoy. I am thankful for all of the wonderful family and friends I have met on this road long traveled.

Pansy in the garden

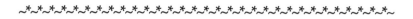

Dear Alison,

I know that at the age of ninety-one, I am nearing the end of the road long traveled. The last door will be closing soon … However, there is one more door to open: the door of heaven, where waiting to welcome me will be Vincent, Garland, Violet, Frances, John, Mother, Daddy, friends from the young-couples class and youth from Fuller Memorial Presbyterian Church, friends from New Hope Presbyterian Church, and perhaps a fifteen-year-old boy named James.